essential careers™

CAREERS IN HOSPITALITY

ERIN STALEY

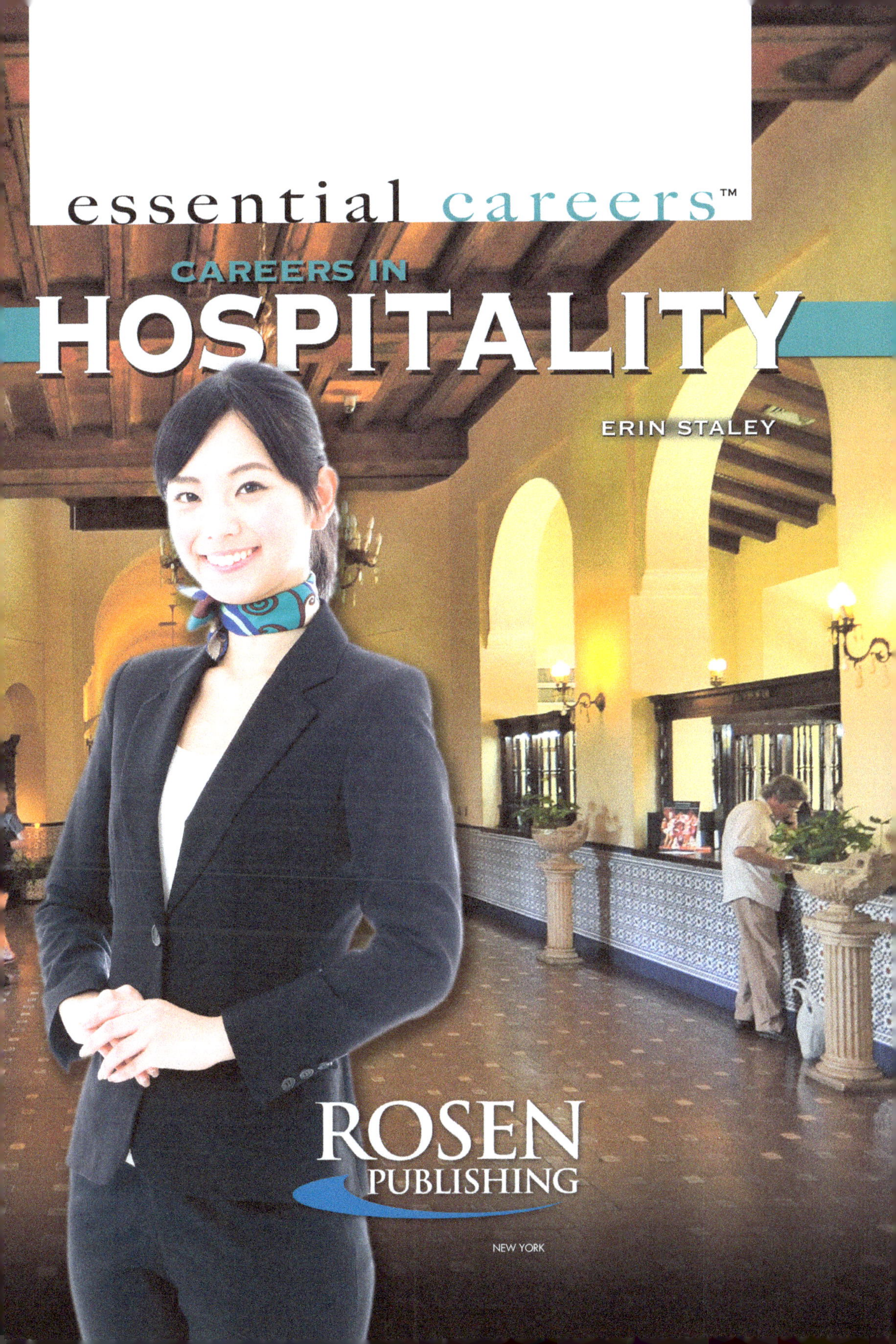

ROSEN PUBLISHING

NEW YORK

Published in 2015 by The Rosen Publishing Group, Inc.
29 East 21st Street, New York, NY 10010

First Edition

Library of Congress Cataloging-in-Publication Data

Staley, Erin.
Careers in hospitality/Erin Staley.
pages cm.—(Essential careers)
Includes bibliographical references and index.
ISBN 978-1-4777-7882-1 (library bound)
1. Hospitality industry—Vocational guidance—Juvenile literature. I. Title.
TX911.3.V62S73 2015
338.4'7910023—dc23

2014010041

Manufactured in the United States of America

contents

INTRO

Jump into a world of possibilities with a career in the hospitality industry. Live, train, and work anywhere as an events, food and beverage, lodging, or travel and tourism specialist.

DUCTION

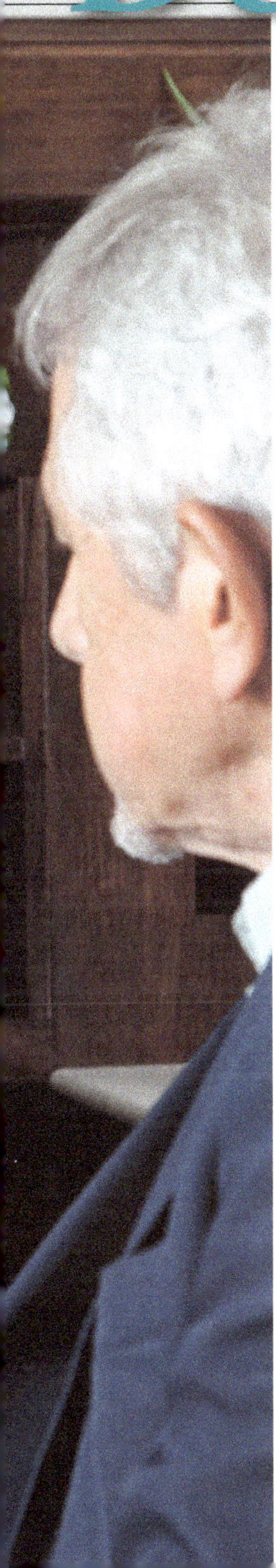

In 2008, the so-called global economic downturn gripped the world economy. News of a threatened stock market hit international airwaves, spreading fear, disappointment, and anxiety. Companies scrambled to "stay in the black" financially. They cut hours, minimized paychecks, limited benefit packages, and laid off employees in order to maintain profitability. Unemployment rates skyrocketed, leaving millions of people in flux; many wondered how their home mortgages, credit cards, and food bills would be paid. It was as if history was repeating itself with a modern-day Great Depression (1929–1939).

Today, we're still feeling the effects of this economic crisis. But it's not just the workforce that is uneasy about its future. Teens sense their parents' worry and observe the community-wide "belt-tightening." They know they may inherit many of these financial burdens; but with eternal optimism, they are ready to do something about it. Teens and young adults are proactive, practicing thrifty principles and financial conservatism, growing their own food and refurbishing what they already have. They are also quite resourceful and self-reliant, especially when it comes to carving out a career path that is long-lasting and secure. The next generation of citizens recognizes the importance of investing their time, energy, and passions into a profession that can leapfrog over difficult economic times. It's all about determining which industry will provide a substantial living, as well as professional growth and personal development. And let's not forget the perks! Health benefits, paid vacations, free travel—these can really sweeten the deal.

Perhaps you're thinking about your professional future—what you'd like to do for the next four or five decades Maybe you'd like to find an outlet for your passion—whipping up scrumptious canapés, welcoming guests onboard, or wowing audiences with your show-stopping moves. If so, keep reading. You'll learn how to turn your passion for serving others into a lucrative, fulfilling, and highly respected career. Introducing. . . the hospitality industry!

The hospitality industry is "the people business." It is one that continues to thrive despite the muck and mire of economic downturns, recessions, and depressions. Did you know that despite the global economic downturn, 12.4 million people work in the hospitality industry? According to the U.S. Bureau of Labor Statistics, the industry added 390,000 jobs and is expected to grow 17 percent through the end of 2014. That's approximately 2.2 million new jobs—favorable statistics for a promising career. So how is it that this industry is so successful? People are looking for ways to escape troubled times and enjoy the more meaningful things in life—dinner with family, a night out on the town with a loved one, or a stress-free getaway. As a professional in the industry, it's your job to serve an unforgettable experience on a silver platter.

As you read, you'll learn about the heart of service and the various subcategories within the hospitality industry. You'll discover what natural skills and educational experiences you'll need, what to expect, how to break into the industry, and with whom to rub elbows. So, if you're in search of a lucrative career, then the vibrant, diverse field of hospitality is waiting for you.

chapter 1

Welcome to the Hospitality Industry

Have you dreamed of working in a spa set against a lush, tropical jungle? Or have you dreamed of managing a skyscraper hotel in a glamorous international city? If you've fantasized about an exciting career with endless opportunities, then perhaps it's time to consider a profession in the hospitality industry. According to *Merriam-Webster*, "hospitality" is defined as the "generous and friendly treatment of visitors and guests." You can find hospitality offered in restaurants and bars, hotels and casinos, and nightclubs and clubhouses all around the world. Wherever people dine, sleep, meet, gamble, or party, you can bet the hospitality industry is in full swing.

The Heart of Service

In order to work in the hospitality industry, one must be able to anticipate a guest's need. Then he or she must be willing to wow the guest with extraordinary service. We call this the "heart of service." Think about your favorite place to eat. Does it have the best food in four states? Now think about your favorite vacation spot. Does it have the most comfortable pillows and the biggest flatscreen televisions? What about your favorite amusement park? Does it have gravity-defying roller coasters that make your heart race and leave you wanting more? Sure, all of these places are top-notch with great menu options, comfortable amenities, and jaw-dropping attractions. But consider this. What if the staff at each location treated you poorly? What if the server ignored your table, or the hotel housekeeper left dirty sheets on your bed? What if the ticket taker kept your change after you paid your park admission? Would their lack of heart-filled service change your mind about returning? Absolutely. You wouldn't go back to any of these locations if the customer service was poor.

A heart of service makes for outstanding customer service. It causes the guest to feel special, and in turn, tell others about the experience. In fact, a happy customer could become your best promoter with word-of-mouth advertising. He would tell his friends, neighbors, family, coworkers, and the online community about your organization. They, in turn, would consider your organization for their next dining, travel, or amusement park adventure. This level of service is extremely valuable to any establishment, as happy customers make for higher profits. Industry employers are willing to pay well for outstanding hospitality representatives who extend a heart of service.

JOB SECURITY IN AN EVER-CHANGING ECONOMY

The worldwide economy has had its fair share of downturns, recessions, and even depressions. Despite these ups and downs, people continue to travel, dine out, and seek entertainment opportunities. That is why a career in the hospitality industry

Say "bon voyage" to a boring, lifeless job. It's time to jump-start your career aboard a cruise ship bound for any number of the world's most exotic destinations.

is considered one of the more enduring professions. If you are good at what you do, you will always have professional opportunities no matter where you want to live in the world. If you see yourself as one who is passionate and motivated to make every guest's experience second to none, then a promising career in the hospitality industry could be yours.

MAKING THE DREAM A REALITY

The hospitality industry is often described as a giant umbrella with four subcategories: events, food and beverage, lodging, and travel and tourism. Oftentimes, these subcategories intertwine, offering you endless opportunities to thrive as a hospitality professional.

PUT ON A SHOW WITH THE EVENTS INDUSTRY

Working in the events field is one of the most electrifying careers in the hospitality industry. It's a "start with nothing and create something extraordinary" option that is perfect for those who prefer a hands-on approach. For example, you could coordinate weddings for a quaint seaside bed and breakfast. Or you could plan a three-day convention for billion-dollar companies in an urban setting. You could also organize a must-see rock show in a trendy concert hall. The sky's the limit if you like to put on the show.

"BON APPETIT" WITH FOOD AND BEVERAGE

From fast-food joints to fancy five-star restaurants, the food and beverage profession is a flourishing industry. Who doesn't love to eat and drink delicious concoctions? You may even like to create your own. As a food and beverage enthusiast, you could turn your passion into a career. Become a chef, restaurant manager, catering supervisor, or food and beverage director for various establishments. Of course, you could even venture into the specialty categories of this

Love music? Consider a career as a concert promoter. You'll need a keen sense of business, sharp multitasking skills, and an excitement for bringing audiences to their feet.

Wow guests with innovative flavors and creative flair as an executive chef. Enroll in any number of world-class culinary schools and get the training you need to serve up excellence.

industry and work in pubs, bars, and nightclubs or with privately owned catering companies. In fact, one such specialty category has taken the world by storm. Coffee shops have become a phenomenon within the industry. According to the coffee and espresso industry website E-Imports, there were approximately twenty-four thousand coffee shops in the United States in 2013. By 2014, that number was expected to climb sharply, hitting the fifty thousand mark. This increase means that there will be more barista positions for those who are eager to brew exotic coffee blends and immerse themselves in the café scene.

HIT THE JACKPOT WITH A CAREER IN THE GAMING INDUSTRY

Lights. Glamour. Money. It's all a part of the gaming industry, and it's an exciting career opportunity for those who like life in the fast lane. If you're a "people person," you could opt for an entry-level position in a casino betting shop, bingo hall, or horse and dog track. The gaming industry comes with three benefits: it does not require previous work experience, pre-employment training is provided, and you could work your way up the corporate ladder rather quickly because the gaming industry has a high turnover rate. According to David Schwartz, director of the Center for Gaming Research at the University of Nevada Las Vegas, "Casinos tend to have a higher turnover rate than hospitality in general, which also is a higher turnover rate than the U.S. job market in general." Schwartz believes this is due to the demands of working shifts and dealing with customers who may have lost hundreds or thousands of dollars. This could be improved, Schwartz notes, if casinos were to better prepare their new employees and maintain company-wide motivation. But for those who can stay enthused about the job—and the entertainment aspect of the industry—a thrilling career awaits. Just think of it: You could be a casino pit boss in charge of gaming tables, or you could give odds and take bets on sporting events as a bookmaker. Then there are the behind-the-scenes positions: chefs, bartenders, janitors, or security officials. And if you have an interest in making sure players and casinos follow gambling regulations, you could always become a highly regarded gaming inspector.

SWEET DREAMS WITH THE LODGING INDUSTRY

Whether you work in a cozy youth hostel or the most glamorous all-inclusive resort in the area, the success of your establishment comes down to making people feel at home. No longer is it just a place for guests to rest their heads. No, the lodging industry is a bustling all-day and all-night business. Today, guests book their reunions, weddings, anniversaries, bar mitzvahs, and holiday parties at accommodations around the world. Plus, they are keen on using the amenities of the establishment, including the spa, workout room, business center, pool, and gardens. With so much to offer, proprietors need to have well-qualified hospitality professionals to oversee every aspect of the guests' experience. They may need to hire a general manager, event coordinator, housekeeping director, reservations specialist, kitchen porter, human resources administrator, entertainment performer, spa manager, gym director, or sales team executive.

AROUND THE WORLD WITH TRAVEL AND TOURISM

Millions of international travelers flock to museums, zoos, amusement parks, fairgrounds, and seaside attractions each year. As a hospitality professional working in this field, it would be your job to make sure everyone has fun. This means you could entertain history buffs as you take them on tour in a world-renowned museum. Or you could put on an aquatic show with whales and dolphins as a part of the training team at a local marine park. Whatever you choose to do, you will have an abundance of career opportunities in this subcategory. Why? Because it's growing by leaps and bounds. A report

Tour guides enhance the museum experience by sharing interesting information about displayed items. They also respond to questions, distribute brochures, and offer audiovisual presentations.

published by the World Travel & Tourism Council (WTTC) notes the industry created over four million new jobs in 2012. This was attributed to international visitors who have an "appetite for travel beyond national borders." On a worldwide scale, travel and tourism's economic contribution reached "9 percent of the global GDP (US $6.6 trillion) and generated over 260 million jobs—1 in 11 of the world's total jobs. The industry outperformed the entire wider economy in 2012, growing faster than other notable industries, such as manufacturing, financial services and retail." WTTC experts believe the travel and tourism industry's future is bright. They predict that by 2023, the number of jobs in this sector will reach 337.8 million.

chapter 2

SERVICE WITH A SMILE

These days anything and everything can be bought with the click of a mouse. So why do customers still jump in their cars and drive down to local retail shops to make purchases? They want the total brand experience. Smart marketers like Apple, Costco, and the Walt Disney

A key aspect of the hospitality industry is smiling. The simple act of smiling greatly impacts customers and keeps them coming back to your restaurant, store, or hotel.

Company know this and go out of their way to make customers feel at home with their outstanding service. The key to success? Always provide service with a smile. Did you know that the simple act of smiling can greatly impact the customer's overall experience? Endorphins—feel-good hormones—are immediately released into the body. If a customer feels good, he or she is more likely to buy. Plus, smiling is contagious. When you smile, your customers smile, too. So as a hospitality specialist, one of your best tried-and-true skills is service with a smile. Once you have mastered this element of service, you can go on to share your other natural skills with the general public.

The Show Must Go On

To be successful in the events industry, you'll need to have excellent organizational and communication skills. As a site crew member, you'll be expected to come to work with a good attitude, listen carefully to what is expected of you, and be able to handle any situation. Sometimes the pressure of work-related catastrophes can be daunting. Maybe the guest of honor is running an hour late, or maybe your team is short-staffed. Perhaps there were some last-minute additions to the program or mechanical breakdowns with the sound system. These things happen. However, you'll need to be cool, calm, and collected while on the job. If you can stay levelheaded and reach a workable solution, then you'll become a highly valued member of the team.

As you gain experience, you can take on greater professional responsibilities. This typically means that eventually, you could

Welcome participants to conferences and trade shows as a convention service manager. You'll need excellent communication and organizational skills, as well as an ability to stay composed under pressure.

coordinate your own events from start to finish. Tasks would range from choosing a venue to creating a guest list and from reviewing supplier contracts to adhering to corporate, state, and national health and safety regulations. This means that you will need to have your details in working order and be flexible when things go wrong. And they will go wrong. Inevitably, you'll have no-shows, cancellations, and weather-related snafus. Take, for instance, Mike Shea, executive director for the South by Southwest (SXSW) annual conference and festival in Texas. He often works with thousands of event details each year: 49,000 conference attendees; 2,098 music festival showcases, 1,221 conference sessions, 1,096 exhibit spaces, and 293 film festival screenings. According to an online *U.S. News & World Report* article, Shea recalled an occasion when he had to think on his feet:

> One year, massive downpours turned a grassy park into muck and mire, threatening two days of free concerts. We decided to blanket the park with hay, and we paced the park from end to end and arbitrarily determined that 10 steps equaled one bale of hay. To remove the muddy hay afterwards, our solution was [to use] homeless men with pitchforks...

Shea used imagination to solve the "muck and mire" problem. He effectively communicated with his team, and together they took additional time to implement the solution. Event planning is being willing to do what it takes—for as long as it takes—because in the end, the "show must go on."

THE FOOD CHAIN

The food and beverage industry is built on exceptional service and unforgettable foods. It's a 24/7 industry, and shift

FROM WOOLEN UNDERWEAR TO A LODGING DYNASTY

A Utah farm boy, John Willard Marriott Sr. (1900–1985), got his start in entrepreneurship at age thirteen. He started a summer lettuce business, which brought in a whopping $2,000, big money in those days. Although successful, Marriott dreamed of a life beyond the farm. He didn't have a high school diploma, but he knew that a college education would help him achieve his entrepreneurial goals. He sold woolen underwear to lumberjacks and earned enough money to attend college. The next step? To secure an A&W Root Beer franchise for Washington, D.C.

In the spring of 1927, Marriott headed east. Together with his partner, Hugh Colton, they collected the needed $6,000 for equipment and space. On May 20, 1927, the entrepreneurial duo opened a nine-stool root beer stand. Marriott expanded his business with the Hot Shoppe eateries. He was incredibly hands-on, getting involved in every aspect of his ventures. Eventually his son took over, and started Marriott International, Inc., one of the largest lodging companies in the world. Today, there are over 3,700 properties—ranging from limited-service to full-service luxury hotels and resorts—in over seventy-three countries and territories.

Although retired, Marriott Sr. continued to visit his hotel locations, maintaining his hands-on management style. The trademark of his management was spending time with Marriott associates. In his opinion, these team members were the secret of his company's success. He believed the keystone of his company's culture was, "Take care of your employees and they'll take care of your customers." To this day, Marriott International, Inc., is considered to be a top employer. Among its endless employment awards, the corporation claimed the fifty-seventh spot on *Fortune* magazine's "100 Best Companies to Work For" list in 2014.

Skills can be learned, but passion can't be faked. If you have a passion for service, consider an extraordinary career in the food and beverage industry.

work is common. As a new employee, you will be asked to work odd hours, often filling in during slow shifts. This will give you time to master the behind-the-scenes protocol: memorizing the menu, getting familiar with cleanup procedures, and following a long list of health and safety regulations. As you improve, you could be invited to work during busier shifts. These are always in high demand among waitstaff because it comes with higher tip-earning potential. Eventually, you could work your way up to becoming an assistant, general, or regional manager. Or perhaps you will decide to start your own food and beverage business, attend culinary school, or buy a franchise.

In order to move up the "food chain," one has to be a people person. Whether you are a server or manager, a dishwasher or head chef, a bartender or sommelier, you'll likely come face-to-face with customers who will expect you to be friendly, attentive, and knowledgeable. And like the other subcategories under the hospitality umbrella, this is especially true when things do not run smoothly. There will be times when reservations are lost, food is late, drinks are spilled, and overtime is expected because half of your team came down with the cold. This will require a respectful attitude and thick skin should a guest decide to show you how unhappy he or she really is. But as a food and beverage specialist, you'll become a calm problem-solver, ready to offer a resolution that meets the need and fits within the framework of your organization's policies. This dedication to turn a negative situation into a positive experience will make all the difference for your guests—and for your career.

A GREAT REFUGE

George Bernard Shaw once said, "The great advantage of a hotel is that it's a great refuge from home life." And his words couldn't be more accurate. People love to get away from home and stay in all sorts of accommodations, from small and quaint to large and luxurious. Bed and breakfasts, boutique hotels, and youth hostels—these are all examples of smaller accommodations in the lodging industry. Each offers a unique set of career opportunities that allows you to get to know your guests up close and personal. For example, if you're on staff at a bed and breakfast, you may be asked to juggle many customer-related responsibilities at one time. This could include everything from chopping fresh, locally grown ingredients to

A maid today, a janitorial business owner tomorrow! Exciting opportunities await as you make those vacation homes, commercial sites, and post-construction properties shine!

handling an emergency toilet repair in a guest room. Expect to be on duty during weekends and holidays, especially if your establishment relies on seasonal bookings. These are the busiest times for the hospitality industry in general.

Of course, there are larger accommodations for guests who want extravagant amenities. These can include high-rise hotels and expansive resorts. Because of their size, larger lodging facilities tend to have individual departments, which focus on specific services within the organization. These include reception, room service, housekeeping, and security. As an entry-level employee, you could find yourself working in one of these departments. If you were a bellboy loading and delivering suitcases, you would work for reception. If you were a poolside server, serving snack food and umbrella-decorated drinks, you would work for the food and beverage department.

But bear in mind that there are certain standards that you'll

Live and work at your dream destination. Use your hospitality skills to welcome guests to the charm and culture of faraway lands.

need to uphold no matter the size of lodging accommodation. Because you're likely to come face to face with guests on a daily basis, you will need to have a positive attitude, great communication skills, and a willingness to take on new challenges. Your employer will depend on you to solve customer service problems and preserve the client relationship. Plus, you will need to uphold all hygiene, safety, and security standards set forth by your employer, the government, and the hospitality industry. Your customers' health and safety are of the utmost importance, so making sure they have an incident-free time at your lodging location will make for many happy returns (and tips).

If you would like to further your career, senior-level positions will become available. Positions such as department manager or general manager will offer more responsibility in exchange for a better paycheck and benefit package. All you need is on-the-job experience, excellent reviews from your supervisors, additional training certification, and a willingness to do whatever it takes to provide "a great refuge" for your guests.

The travel and tourism industry has employment opportunities in every corner of the world—even in the friendly skies! Watch your career "take off" as a highly trained flight attendant.

THINK ON YOUR FEET

Just like the other hospitality subcategories, you'll need to demonstrate a wide range of natural abilities to be an outstanding travel and tourism professional. However, if you want to stand out, you'll need to have cultural sensitivity. Inevitably, guests from various countries will want to frequent your lodging property, travel agency, cruise line, tour business, or car rental firm. And it'll be important for you to consider their language and customs when offering assistance. For example, if you were a flight attendant, you would have passengers who speak a different language. You would have to think on your feet in order to help them with luggage, gate information, emergency procedures, and even dinner options. But perhaps this will inspire you to learn a second, third, or fourth language. It never hurts to have additional skills to bring to the table when searching out advancement opportunities.

The travel and tourism subcategory also requires shift work. You will need to be on hand during busy times to book reservations, give directions, and point out the particulars of a must-see attraction. But if you're willing to work evenings, weekends, and holidays, then the benefits will far outweigh the sometimes inconvenient hours. One benefit is the opportunity to travel for business—either at discounted rates or for free. This is possible if you're a cruise director, managing travel agent, or tour manager. Also, attending workshops and conferences could enhance your training, taking your knowledge to the next level. Another benefit, if you see it as such, is the chance to move to a new location without advance notice. These opportunities often come with promotions, so if you're an adventure seeker, a new city, state, or country might be a huge step up for your career. If you are selected for management in the travel and tourism industry, you could likely create staffing schedules; hire, fire, and train employees; work up a yearly budget; order supplies; analyze profitability; create and implement promotions; and cater to unhappy customers. Or you could specialize within the industry. For example, you could be a member of the marketing team. Your job would be to create a strategy to attract domestic and overseas visitors to your organization.

As a marketing specialist, you'd be thinking of ways to bring in more profitability to an already well-established industry. It's interesting to note the lodging industry has had a profound economic impact on the economy. In 2013, the American Hotel & Lodging Association (AH&LA) concluded, "Resident and international travelers in the United States spend an average of $2.3 billion a day, $97.6 million an hour, $1.6 million a minute, and $27,125 a second." In fact, the AH&LA noted the industry employs 1.8 million hotel property workers and "directly supports more than 7.7 million travel and tourism jobs." This, of course, affects the world as travelers rack up more international travel miles than ever before. You can be a part of this adventure with a promising career in the fast-paced and constantly changing industry of travel and tourism.

chapter 3

GETTING STARTED IN THE HOSPITALITY INDUSTRY

By now, you're probably thinking the hospitality industry could be a good fit for you. Maybe you've said to yourself, "Wow, I could work in this industry, doing what I love and having the chance to meet new people and travel the world." And why not? You have the natural abilities—honesty, patience, and respect for others—needed for this type of employment. You work well as a team player and can effectively solve problems with creativity and flexibility. All you need is a little help in getting started. In this section, we're going to look at venues that will give you the required education and training to help you reach your professional goals.

Doing well in school is always a great way to begin your professional journey. However, you don't have to be a straight-A student to enjoy a long, prosperous career in the hospitality industry. Potential candidates will have to prove that they are capable of producing quality results, meeting deadlines, and keeping tardies and absences to a minimum. Employers and hiring managers want to fill their entry-level positions with well-rounded, responsible candidates. Often teenagers are able to work part-time in the hospitality industry while they're earning their high school diploma. They are able to get their foot in the door as servers in fast-food and dine-in restaurants, ticket

Oftentimes a career in hospitality starts with an entry-level position, such as a ticket taker at a movie theater. But with time and great service, you can quickly move up the ladder.

takers at local cinemas, janitors at amusement parks, or landscapers at the local country club.

The type and size of your chosen organization may determine how much experience and education is needed for a management position. It all boils down to what you want to do. If you want to run a small lodge with sixty guest rooms or less, a high school diploma and a few years of experience may be all you need. However, if you've set your sights on something much grander—say a luxury resort with over four hundred rooms—you'll need at least a bachelor's degree and five years of on-the-job experience.

Getting a Leg Up with Vocational-Technical Programs

Many students decide to get a leg up on professional competition by enrolling in vocational-technical (vo-tech) programs. Most of these work-based programs are part-time for high school students. Alternatively, some students choose to attend full-time vo-tech high schools. The typical school day is divided between technical training (such as electronics and the culinary arts) and a nationally recognized academic curriculum (including subjects such as English, math, physical education, science, and social studies).

Enhance your career by attending industry workshops and conferences. You may be giving up some free time, but the payoff will be long-lasting: knowledge, skills, and the boss's attention.

As vo-tech students become more proficient in their technical skills, they can apply what they've learned while working in related businesses. This is true for hospitality-related training. Eventually, students must pass industry exams to graduate. Every state has its own testing criteria, but most contain the same kind of benchmarks. First comes the academic skills. Students need to have a basic knowledge of everything from creating and proofreading professional documents to calculating percentages and developing financial budgets. Second is the general workplace skills assessment. School officials must be convinced that students are able to find a job using proper interview techniques, successfully complete assigned tasks on their own, develop and analyze presentations, and display good work habits. Leadership skills are particularly important in this section. Vocational students have to prove they can lead a team, analyze the effectiveness of new hires, provide quality customer service, create a pleasant working environment, and minimize losses

Kaimuki High School

According to an article in the *Washington Post*, "Visitors spent more than $14 billion in Hawaii in 2012," making tourism "the largest single contributor to the state's gross domestic product." Unfortunately, Hawaii's hospitality workforce is aging. Within five years, over ten thousand employees are expected to retire. In response to the upcoming job vacancies, Kaimuki High School created the Hookipa Workforce Academy. Its purpose? To train teenagers for the entry-level jobs in Hawaii's hospitality industry.

In the summer of 2013, school officials tested the program with twenty-six seniors. Half of the day was spent on academic skills—reading, writing, and arithmetic—that related to their summer occupation. The other half of the day was spent performing vocational duties, such as filling fast-food orders, planting turf, or changing hotel linens. Students were expected to punch in ten minutes early and wear work uniforms. When they punched out at the end of the day, they took with them a paycheck, improved confidence, and hiring preference when it came time to apply for post–high school hospitality employment. Civilbeat.com notes that often basic industry skills are lacking among people in entry-level positions. It follows with the observations of program founder and local businessman, Brian Keala Benz:

> [But with those skills,] "the hospitality industry just becomes more powerful, providing even better service . . . and you make people feel rewarded for the work that they do, proud of

what they do so it's no longer a chore but rather a good way of living."

At the conclusion of the program, the Hookipa Workforce Academy was declared a success. Future Kaimuki students were set to enjoy the benefits as the innovative program was slotted to continue to run full force through the 2014–2015 school year.

Talk to your guidance counselor about the travel and tourism industry. Learn what it takes to become an eco-friendly tour guide, an all-inclusive resort concierge, or a restaurant owner.

or liabilities. The third category of testing is the vocational skills. Students need to show that they can research and analyze information within the industry and stay up on industry trends. Finally, students must be able to demonstrate broad technical skills. They should be able to operate job-related technology, work according to job safety and security procedures, and effectively perform across a broad range of industry occupations. Once these tests are passed with flying colors, vo-tech students are awarded a high school diploma and technical certification. They are now career-ready, which

Invest in your future by enrolling in any of a number of internationally acclaimed schools. Gain the skills you need to serve others and significantly boost your future earning power.

gives them a "leg up" over other high school–only candidates. Many receive multiple job offers with pay well over minimum wage. Of course, some vo-tech graduates enroll in secondary institutions to further their career options—and increase their earning power.

HIGHER EDUCATION = STRONGER EARNING POWER

Professionals who are already working full-time in the travel and tourism industry often go back to school part-time to earn an advanced degree. Why? Because they know the bigger payoff comes with advanced training. If you want to fast-track your career, consider earning an associate's, bachelor's, or master's degree in hospitality management. Whether your niche is restaurant, event, resort club, or casino management, you will have an even wider range of skills and competencies to attract future employers. In fact, some athletic teams prefer to hire event organizers with a degree in hospitality management. Why? Because these hospitality professionals have the know-how to effectively plan travel and living arrangements for their athletes.

Across the nation, there are hundreds of hospitality management programs from which to choose. They offer the standard prerequisite courses, as well as recommended hospitality classes for your area of interest. Some have you dive right in, taking classes in your major during the first term. Hospitality faculty members present theory and management techniques while drawing lessons from their own work experience. Plus, top-of-the-line industry tools and software are at your fingertips as you

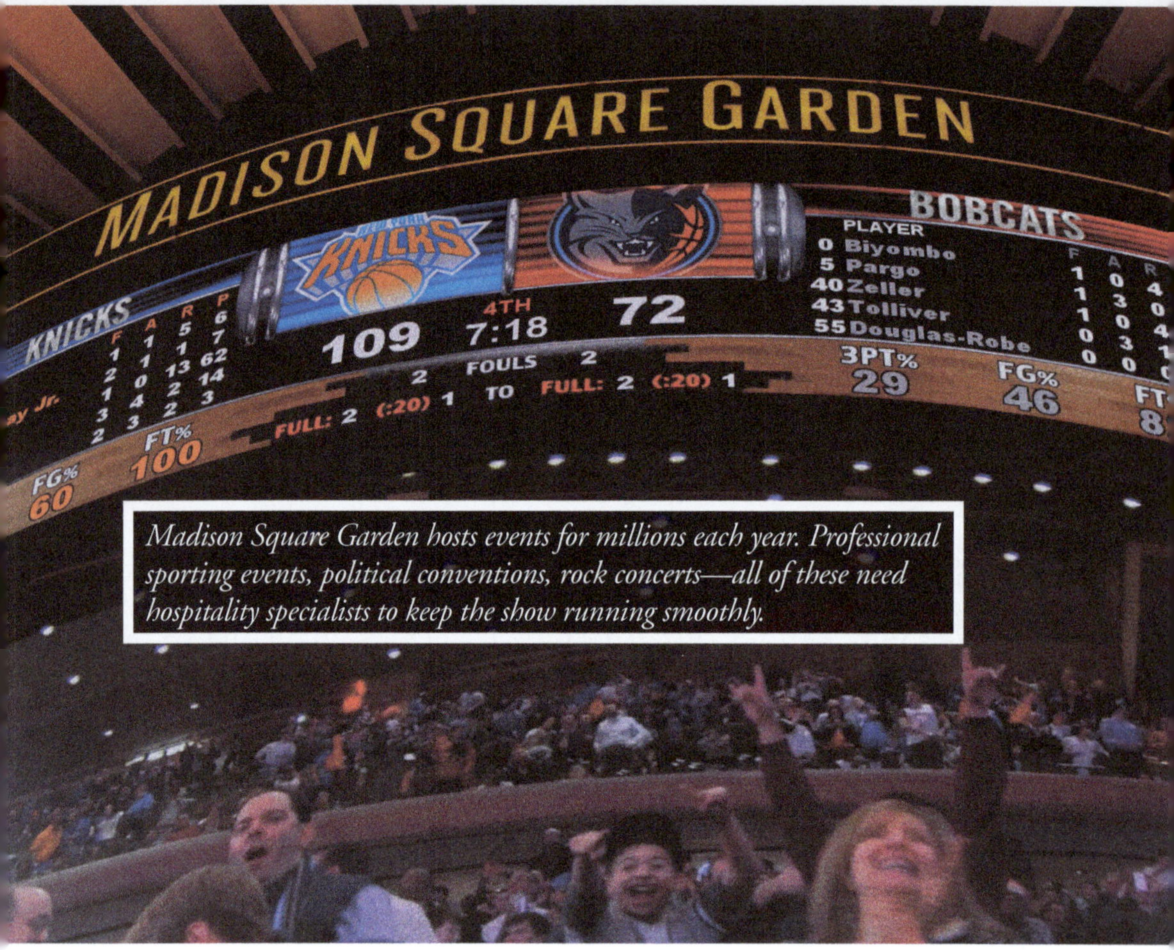

Madison Square Garden hosts events for millions each year. Professional sporting events, political conventions, rock concerts—all of these need hospitality specialists to keep the show running smoothly.

complete assignments in their classrooms, event spaces, and labs. Many educational institutions have teamed up with leading employers to give their students a hands-on experience. Hospitality hopefuls can participate in national and international internship programs with employers such as Royal Caribbean, Madison Square Garden, Ritz-Carlton, and ESPN. Not only do you get to do what you love, but you also get to live it for a term. Internships let you put your learning into action while earning academic credit and making global connections. You may even have a job offer by the time you graduate.

chapter 4

At Your Service

You've earned your high school diploma, vo-tech certification, and sparkling new college degree. You're armed with a can-do attitude and a readiness to create an extraordinary experience for your guests. Now you're ready to land your dream job.

The Job Search

If you're looking to charge up your career as a top hospitality professional, there are several must-dos to consider. First, talk with guests, employees, and hiring managers. They will tell you which companies have a good reputation and which companies to avoid. If you live in a small town, check out the local restaurants, bars, nightclubs, country clubs, lodging accommodations, and convention halls. If you find yourself coming up empty-handed, consider a larger community. Urban areas tend to have more opportunities for job seekers. New York, Los Angeles, Toronto, and Vancouver, for example, attract millions of travelers each year who need a place to stay, eat, and play. And don't forget to look beyond your borders for international opportunities. Of course, the international job market is more competitive than ever. But with determination and professionalism, you could have an illustrious career working in Europe, Asia, South America, or Africa.

During your job search, be sure to visit sites such as LinkedIn. There, you can find a professional job-hunting network that caters to millions of members in more than two hundred countries. It's interesting to note that job seekers aren't the only ones to check

Sun-drenched beaches, snow-capped ski slopes, twirling roller coasters, and spirited urban escapes—travel and tourism will take your breath away as you explore the world.

out LinkedIn. Corporate and agency recruiters often scroll through LinkedIn's résumé database to find mid- to senior-level candidates. While you're there, be sure to look at the site's long list of career-related articles. You might pick up some industry tidbits that could

THE HOSPITALITY INDUSTRY NEVER SLEEPS

As the sun goes down, the night scene comes alive. Restaurants, bars, cabarets, and nightclubs are filled with those who want to wind down by lighting up the town! The energy is electric, and it stays this way long after the clock strikes midnight. It's all a part of the nightlife scene—a special category under the hospitality umbrella that continues to pump up the economy and employ countless hospitality professionals. According to the U.S. Census Bureau's Statistics of U.S. Businesses, there were approximately "351,912 people employed within the industry with nearly $4.1 billion in annual payroll in 2005." Furthermore, the Nightlife & Club Industry Association of America (NCIAA) notes findings that state, "Sales of spirits, wine and beer in licensed on-premise locations increased 4.9 percent to reach $93.7 billion in 2011 and projections call for continued growth up to 2015." From this, we know that the industry is booming, and it's a strong consideration if you're looking for a lucrative, long-term career.

So what makes the nightlife hospitality scene so successful? Sure, the scrumptious food and beverages, thumping dance music, and plush VIP seating are very impressive, but take a moment to think about what's going on behind the scenes. The workforce of bartenders, managers, chefs, servers, bussers, and even security personnel are on hand to take care of any issues before you even notice. Their job is to keep the party going without missing a beat. Plus, it doesn't hurt if they have a little charisma to keep loyal clientele coming in night after night, week after week. If you're energetic, friendly, and can work efficiently with loud music and chatty crowds

around you, then the nightlife scene could be right up your alley. To break into this industry, you'll need to take on the traditional entry-level roles of any other subcategory under the hospitality umbrella, but advancement awaits if you develop a work-quick and work-smart ability. For example, if you're a bartender, you'll want to mix and serve as fast and as accurately as possible. Why? Because your efficiency could significantly affect sales and profitability. If you prove yourself willing and capable, you could become an assistant, general, or regional manager and possibly relocate to the world's biggest and best nightlife cities. From Montreal to Madrid and Buenos Aires to Bangkok, the world could be your hospitality oyster.

The nightclub scene is demanding. Not only will you need to keep the party going, but you'll need to manage administrative duties while staying ahead of the competition.

impress a future interviewer. Other employment websites, such as Indeed and SimplyHired, give free advice on job-hunting basics. For example, they will teach you how to create an attention-getting cover letter and how to properly format your résumé. If you have a particular niche you'd like to target in your search, check out Idealist for nonprofit and volunteer groups, and USAJobs for federal employment openings.

Another way to secure work is by reaching out to a third-party agency. For example, an employment agency will give you professional tips while their recruiters search for employment options to match your skill set. Once a position is secured, you'll likely become a temporary employee. In addition, a service fee will be charged. Recruitment agencies work a little differently. They are contracted by the client. When this client comes to the agency with a particular employment vacancy, the recruiter will access his or her network of prescreened candidates. These candidates will have already passed the required benchmarks—reference checks, background checks, drug testing, and skill analysis. Once the recruiter has the top-qualifying candidates on a short list, the client may select the best fit for the position. If you're selected, you're in for some good news: the job is yours, permanently, and the client pays the service fee.

Professional Hospitality Associations

Hospitality organizations can help you launch your successful career, especially as a student. These groups represent every subcategory under the hospitality umbrella. For example, those working in lodging can join AH&LA. Those in food and beverages can join Foodservice Consultants Society International (FCSI). For a membership fee, these groups provide a wealth of benefits for their members: free legal consultations, credit card partnerships for small businesses, professional magazine subscriptions, discounted

ETHICS IN THE HOSPITALITY INDUSTRY

The hospitality industry, while an exciting business area, is highly competitive. If a customer isn't happy with his or her experience, he or she will spend their money somewhere else. That is why it is crucial for hospitality associates—from entry-level employees to senior-level executives—to maintain a high standard of excellence. This includes work ethics—the values we place on our work.

Accountability. Hospitality associates must be personally accountable for their decisions and actions.

Respect. Employers want to work with team members who respect the organization and its property, as well as the customers and their personal belongings.

Honesty. Team members are expected to be upfront and honest at all times. Deception of any kind is not tolerated.

Integrity. As a staff member, one must demonstrate the courage of his or her conviction, doing what is right despite peer pressure.

Loyalty. Working with a sense of duty to the employer and fellow team members brings cohesion to the organization. This means working without conflict and keeping all business-related information confidential.

registration for industry conventions, and even voting rights for organization leaders. Students are invited to take full advantage of everything the associations have to offer: networking with property owners and managers, and access to valuable resources, employment databases, and exclusive discounts on school supplies and industry event admission. If you network efficiently, you can

Get your interview off on the right foot with a polished appearance and welcoming smile. This, along with a well-written résumé, will speak volumes regarding your professionalism.

even have your résumé circulated among key industry people. With connections like these, you will make a name for yourself and stand out from the crowd. As an added bonus, some hospitality associations like the American Hotel & Lodging Educational Foundation (AH&LEF) award thousands of dollars' worth of scholarships to help with educational pursuits.

Putting Your Best Foot Forward

If you're ready to leapfrog over other candidates who are vying for your dream job, then you must come prepared. Preparation is the key to success, and this can be applied to your professional image, résumé, and nonverbal communication. Your appearance says a lot about the way you see yourself and the level of respect you have for the position you seek. Show your future employer that you mean business by dressing the part. Whether you are interviewing to be a server or a manager, wear a suit. The point is to dress the part of the dream job you want, no matter the position for which you're applying. Someday you may want to be the vice president of operations, and what does that person wear? A suit. Don't forget to tend to every detail, such as your hair, nails, and accessories.

The next thing to consider is your résumé. Be sure that it is as polished as your appearance. If you don't have a long list of work experience, simply reveal your heart of service, enthusiasm, and ability to anticipate the needs of the clients. Only include accurate details, and be sure to review your résumé for typos. A simple spelling error could tarnish your professional appearance. Make several copies of your résumé, and place them in an attractive portfolio.

Nonverbal communication will play a big role in your professional endeavors. The famous American poet Ralph Waldo Emerson once said, "What you are speaks so loudly that I cannot hear what you say." His wisdom can be applied to the concept of first impressions. According to Alyson Krueger of the website Business Insider, applicants have only seven to seventeen seconds to make an unforgettable first impression. Ninety-eight percent of judgments are made on nonverbal communication—posture, facial expressions, and body language. The site goes on to explain that impressions are based on 55 percent physical appearance, 38 percent voice quality (your volume, tone, pitch, and speed), and 7 percent the words that you speak. Successful professionals use all three to convey confidence and competency. They avoid slouching, fidgeting, and crossing their arms in front of their chest. They always arrive early for the interview and are sure to silence their mobile device and tuck it away. In addition, successful professionals make eye contact and offer a warm smile with a firm handshake. Bear in mind that if you're interviewing internationally, say in Southern Europe, Central America, or South America, a lighter, lengthier handshake is more appropriate. As the interview continues, listen attentively and use a polite, conversational tone when it's your turn to speak. After the interview, send a thank-you note or e-mail to the interviewer. Be genuine and be brief, but don't forget to double-check for typos and grammatical errors.

Through it all, simply remember that your attitude will play a major role in the employer's decision-making process. Don't be afraid to let your enthusiasm shine through, and you will not only bring in a paycheck, but you will also bring home the satisfaction of nailing the interview.

chapter 5

Career Advancement

Congratulations! You've been offered a job! You're now ready to roll up your sleeves, learn all you can, and make a difference in your new organization. But don't worry if you don't pick up all of the rules and regulations on the first day. Many employers have trainers or trainee programs to help their newest employees learn the necessary skills to be effective. These on-the-job coaches will teach you in-house procedures, show you where to put your belongings, give you a tour of the facility, and help with any employment forms—payment, health care benefits, and taxation—you will need. Don't be shy about asking questions, as your trainers are there to help you be your best. While you pay your dues, look for opportunities to get more involved within your industry. Volunteer to be on special development teams or help with the company's annual charity ball. Get involved and you'll learn more than you could think was possible. Further demonstrate your willingness to be a part of the team by finding a mentor or professional coach within your organization or among industry "movers and shakers." They will guide you on your career path, offering how-to tips and constructive feedback.

"Rubbing Elbows"

As you become a highly skilled expert in the hospitality industry, be sure to search out networking opportunities when

HOSPITALITY THE WALT DISNEY WAY

The Walt Disney Company is a legend in the hospitality industry. For nearly a century, its approach to customer satisfaction has won over millions of young and "young-at-heart" guests. How do they do it? They use a number of tried-and-true practices. First, the Disney team understands that customers want to feel special. They train their employees—otherwise known as cast members—to make every point of contact with the "guest" memorable. This includes being assertively friendly. Cast members are instructed to greet guests by name when possible, volunteer to take a photo, and replace spilled popcorn or ice cream cones.

Second, cast members work with the four points of the Disney Compass in mind. Walt Disney loved compasses and used north, west, south, and east in his customer service philosophy. "N" stands for "Needs." It represents the meeting of guests' most basic needs. "W" represents "Wants," and allows for an extra level of service. "S" stands for "Stereotypes," overcoming any negative impressions of their business. "E" is for "Emotions" because this is what motivates someone to buy and then come back once the delivery and fulfillment are met.

Third, the Walt Disney Company wows its guests with these seven customer-care guidelines (named after the seven dwarfs in the film *Snow White and the Seven Dwarfs*):

1. **Be Happy.** Make eye contact and smile!

2. **Be like Sneezy.** Greet and welcome each and every guest. Spread the spirit of hospitality, it's contagious!

3. **Don't be Bashful.** Seek out guest contact.

4. Be like Doc. Provide immediate service recovery.

5. Don't be Grumpy. Always display appropriate body language at all times.

6. Be like Sleepy. Create dreams and preserve the "magical" guest experience.

7. Don't be Dopey. Thank each and every guest.

If you're upbeat, reliable, and demonstrate leadership ability, then seek employment opportunities with worldwide corporations. You could rise to new heights as a star employee.

you're at conventions, trade shows, and association events. Networking is "rubbing elbows" with other professionals who are either working in your niche or in other industries altogether. The idea is to develop professional friendships that will provide both short-term and long-term support. With your networking connections, you'll stay up on the latest industry trends and have great access to related resources. Networking is a great way to find a good job, especially if the position isn't advertised traditionally through newspapers and online postings. You can even keep each other "in the loop" by arranging introductions with influential professionals and tipping off one another when openings become available. Networking is an ongoing activity, something you'll continue throughout your professional career. So build a deep network of contacts that can put you in touch with the right people when the right opportunities come along.

THE NEXT STEP

Once you've found your professional stride, there will be times when you may be tempted to think you're in a rut. Maybe your career isn't as exciting as it once was, or maybe each day seems to be an exact replica of the one before. Perhaps you feel as if you're stuck at the same level because you were overlooked for a raise or promotion. But don't fret. Be proactive. Look for ways to go the extra mile. Many employers offer professional development courses, educational webinars, and supplemental training classes for their goal-oriented employees. These continuing education opportunities could be in the form of safety, first-aid, or administrative courses. If your employer does not offer additional training, find out if you can create a committee to do just that. As a committee member, you can implement a new program that will increase the know-how for you and your coworkers. Also, seek outside ways to stay up on the latest resources and knowledge within your industry. This could mean picking up college courses or becoming a member of an industry association. Granted, you may need to participate during your free time, but sacrificing a few evenings and weekends to further educate yourself—and network—could open up a wealth of professional opportunities.

ON YOUR OWN

Once you've gained the necessary experience, you may want to open your own hospitality business. Maybe you've been dreaming of owning a quaint bed and breakfast in the south of France or possibly a hoppin' dance club in the heart of Miami. These are wonderful dreams, but as with anything, it takes a lot of work and a determined mind-set to make them come true.

To get started, you'll need to remember one thing before putting the "We're Open" sign on the door. Remember to practice patience. Starting a business isn't a "get rich quick" scheme. It's a process with a million details to plan and a million more to cross off of your to-do list once you gain some momentum. As long as you set your expectations accordingly, you'll be ready to tackle anything that challenges your goals. Practically speaking, you're also going to need some business know-how. One business key is to give the customers what they want, and they'll respond by giving you their business and recommendations. Another key is to consider where you'll offer your services. Location is everything, and you'll need to select well, especially for the type of products or services you want to offer. For example, if you want to open an upscale restaurant, it would likely not fare well in a one-stoplight town. A larger city may be the right location for this type of business.

Also, choose an area that isn't already saturated by businesses that are too similar to yours. For instance, beware of opening a snack shack in a seaside hideaway when there are

A PEEK INTO HOSPITALITY ENTREPRENEURSHIP

Spending much of her childhood on her grandparents' Oregon farm, Sarah Carlson learned from a young age that every member of her family was quick to share "hospitality on a plate." They lived off the land and were eager to serve guests what they had cooked, baked, butchered, or canned.

In her early twenties, Carlson was introduced to a couple who owned a catering business. They were coordinating a black-tie wedding and desperately needed staff to serve over five hundred guests. She was hired on the spot. On the big day, she stood in the garage-turned-kitchen, mesmerized by the industry in action. She knew this was her dream, but she needed time, money, and experience. Carlson became a full-time manager of a jewelry store where she could fine-tune her business and customer service skills. Meanwhile she continued learning the catering business, working as part-time catering staff. And just like her "hospitality hero," Julia Child, Carlson eventually enrolled in culinary school when she was in her thirties. She graduated from Le Cordon Bleu with honors and started the Red Hare Personal Chef in West Linn, Oregon.

"Nourishing people is very personal; it's my gift to my clients," says Carlson, who incorporates her family's back-to-the-earth lifestyle into her chef business. "Whether I'm making an intimate dinner for two or a large spread for a wedding, I want everyone to feel special and valued by the flavors and quality of my dishes."

As the sole owner, Carlson *is* her business. Not only does she plan, shop, cook, and serve, but she also juggles bookkeeping, advertising, marketing, hiring, transportation, rental coordination, equipment maintenance, and product development. "I'm a 'Jill of all trades,'" says Carlson, "but my most important task is building a relationship with my clients. I have high service standards, and I strive to exceed their expectations. This is the key to success in the hospitality business."

Sarah Carlson and her catering business, the Red Hare Personal Chef, show that personal commitment and passion are key to growing your own endeavor in hospitality.

fifteen other snack shacks in that same destination. Your business will no longer be unique enough to make any money. Avoid this headache by taking the time to research a prime location where you can stand out from the crowd. Then take an objective look at your competitors' prices, quality, and customer service. Can you beat them and continue to make money while offering a top-of-the-line product or service? Next, consider your resources and suppliers. Will you need to have linens shipped in from another country, or can you pick them up locally at a wholesale distributor? But that's not all. You'll need to conform to state and federal regulations to get your business up and running. And once it's making progress, you'll need to determine if you have enough money to attract and hire skilled workers. Then there's the scheduling, security, utilities, paperwork—the list goes on and on. It will take a well-established professional to draw upon his or her experiences and to juggle all of these details. But if you work hard, and pick up tidbits from successful hospitality entrepreneurs around you, you will reach your goals and realize your dream.

NEVER WORK A DAY IN YOUR LIFE

Chinese philosopher Confucius (551–479 BCE) once said, "Choose a job you love,

One key aspect of starting your own business is determining the right location. Many hospitality ventures do best in popular tourist destinations, such as the beach.

A "MARKET BLEND" COMES TO PUERTO VALLARTA, MEXICO

It is common in the hospitality industry for professionals to blend their skills and create something from scratch. This is especially true in the creation of the Old Town Farmers Market-Tianguis Cultural (OTFM-TC). In the summer of 2009, social entrepreneur and Canadian native Charlotte Semple noticed a lack of the "buy local" options she had grown accustomed to in Victoria, British Columbia. She thought a Saturday farmers' market would be a welcome addition to her newly adopted hometown of Puerto Vallarta. It would blend the North American–style market with Mexico's old-world, open-air *tianguis* markets. Semple's "market blend" would not only promote Mexican culture but also pump more money into the local economy, one that had been greatly affected by the global economic downturn of 2008. But tourist season was winding down, and Semple had only two weeks to get the OTFM-TC up and running. She worked tirelessly, securing a location, doing the setup, securing public safety issues, and creating the marketing. She also interviewed would-be vendors who shared her passion for "make it, bake it, grow it" products. Come opening day, the market was a hit, with thirty vendors and nearly eight hundred visitors.

Today, the OTFM-TC is one of Puerto Vallarta's most exciting, must-see weekend attractions. Located in the heart of the city, the market attracts over one hundred thousand national and international shoppers who scoop up everything from farm-fresh produce to artisan crafts. Weekend visitors contribute to on-site nonprofit groups and "eat to the beat," savoring international cuisine and toe-tapping rhythms. They also come for special market events such as the University of Guadalajara's Estación Gourmet. While snacking on fare made by Ministry of Tourism culinary students, visitors listen to Spain's celebrity chef Paco Morales discuss local food production and the global "buy local" movement.

As the OTFM-TC founder and director, Semple continues to oversee the day-to-day administration of the market. This includes determining the market's estimated economic impact. In its 2012–2013 season, the market's impact reached over five million pesos (nearly half a million dollars). Semple also saw to it that donations were given to cultural projects, neighborhood improvement projects, and entrepreneurial development for OTFM-TC vendors. As a result of Semple's efforts to share her hospitality skills, meet a need, and help her community, city officials honored her with the 2012 Association of Residents and Business Owners Community Service Award.

By combining "buy local" elements of American markets with the open-air concept of the Mexican tianguis, *Charlotte Semple's Puerto Vallarta market became a must-see hit with tourists and locals.*

and you will never have to work a day in your life." If serving others in a fast-paced, always-changing environment is something that you love, then consider the dynamic industry of hospitality. Events, food and beverage, lodging, and travel and tourism—the four subcategories of hospitality—are all waiting for you. Avoid the frenzy of those who are scrambling to find profitable work in times of economic uncertainty. Choose a career that continues to thrive. As a specialist in the hospitality industry, you'll earn a lucrative living, meet fascinating people, and see some of the most spectacular sites in the world.

glossary

all-inclusive Describing a resort that includes the service of daily meals, beverages, desserts, and gratuities in the cost.

amenities Features that increase the appeal or value of a property.

benchmark A standard of reference by which a student or employment candidate is assessed.

benefit package Benefits paid to an employee ranging from workers' compensation to unemployment compensation and from health insurance to paid vacation time.

betting shop A licensed bookmaking shop where bets are made.

bookmaker Also known as a "bookie," this person or company helps gamblers bet on a sporting event or horse race.

entrepreneur One who owns and operates a business venture.

entry-level position A job reserved for those with professional qualification but who lack practical experience.

five-star The universally accepted rating for the highest-quality facilities, such as hotels or restaurants.

franchise The right or license to sell an organization's goods or services in a specific region.

human resources The department or office that is responsible for hiring and firing, employment records, and legalities.

lucrative Financially profitable or yielding income.

mentor An industry professional who offers advice and guidance to another.

minimum wage The lowest wage an organization can pay an employee according to the law.

prescreening A method by which one reviews a potential candidate in great detail before making a hiring decision.

sommelier A wine steward who oversees an organization's wine collection and makes pairing recommendations for customers.

third-party agency An independent organization that provides a professional service for businesses.

trade show A special conference designed to feature new products and services for a specific industry.

travel agent One who makes travel arrangements for individuals, groups, or corporations.

turnover rate The total number of employees who have left an organization.

vocational Referring to the special skills and training needed to complete a specific job.

word-of-mouth advertising An oral or written endorsement for a business, product, or service from a satisfied customer.

youth hostel An accommodation for those who travel on a budget, typically students or other young people.

for more information

American Culinary Federation, Inc. (ACF)
180 Center Place Way
St. Augustine, FL 32095
(800) 624-9458
Website: http://www.acfchefs.org
Founded in 1929, the American Culinary Federation was made up of three chefs' organizations: the Société Culinaire Philanthropique, the Vatel Club, and the Chefs de Cuisine Association of America. Today, the ACF promotes the professional reputation of American chefs worldwide through education.

American Hotel & Lodging Association (AH&LA)
1201 New York Avenue NW, Suite 600
Washington, DC 20005
(202) 289-3100
Website: http://www.ahla.com
The AH&LA oversees the legislative, media, educational, research, and public interests of the lodging industry within the United States.

Club Managers Association of America (CMAA)
1733 King Street
Alexandria, VA 22314
(703) 739-9500
Website: http://www.cmaa.org
The CMAA offers resources to managers of membership clubs. It has nearly 6,500 members working in approximately 2,500 athletic, city, country, faculty, golf, military, town, and yacht clubs.

Convention Industry Council (CIC)
700 N. Fairfax Street, Suite 510
Alexandria, VA 22314
(571) 527-3116
Website: http://www.conventionindustry.org
Founded in 1949, the Convention Liaison Council facilitates the exchange of information within the meetings, conventions, and exhibitions industry. It provides a variety of resources to support the industry and its members.

Foodservice Consultants Society International (FCSI)
180 Center Place Way
St. Augustine, FL 32095
(800) 624-9458
Website: http://www.fcsi.org
The FCSI promotes professionalism and offers consulting services for food and beverage professionals in over forty-six countries.

Hotel Association of Canada (HAC)
130 Albert Street, Suite 1206
Ottawa, ON K1P 5G4
Canada
(613) 237-7149
Website: http://www.hotelassociation.ca
For over a century, the Hotel Association of Canada has enhanced the Canadian hotel and lodging industry by representing over 8,500 hotels, motels, and resorts.

International Association of Amusement Parks and Attractions (IAAPA)
1448 Duke Street
Alexandria, VA 22314
(703) 836-4800

Website: http://www.iaapa.org
Founded in 1918, the IAAPA is the largest trade association for permanently situated amusement facilities worldwide. From amusement parks to museums and science centers to water parks, it helps its international membership ensure the safety, development, growth, and success of their establishments.

International Special Events Society (ISES)
330 N. Wabash Avenue, Suite 2000
Chicago, IL 60611
(800) 688-4737
Website: http://www.ises.com
For over twenty-five years, the International Special Events Society has provided inspiration, networking, and education and professional development opportunities for its membership.

National Association for Catering and Events (NACE)
9891 Broken Land Parkway, Suite 301
Columbia, MD 21046
(410) 290-5410
Website: http://www.nace.net
The oldest and largest catering association in the world, the NACE works "to advance the catering and events industry and its professionals." It offers professional certification, educational programs, networking opportunities, community service projects, and annual conferences.

National Restaurant Association (NRA)
2055 L Street NW, Suite 700
Washington, DC 20036
(800) 424-5156
Website: http://www.restaurant.org

The NRA supports almost five hundred thousand restaurant businesses by supporting foodservice industry interests in state, local, and national policies. It also provides help for members with operational, networking, educational, and research resources.

Old Town Farmers Market-Tianguis Cultural (OTFM-TC)
Parque Lazaro Cardenas
Colonia Emiliano Zapata
Puerto Vallarta, JAL, 48300
Mexico
52 (322) 205-3384
Website: http://www.oldtownfm.com
The Old Town Farmers Market-Tianguis Cultural is a North American–style market that celebrates the tradition of Mexico's *tianguis* markets. It offers "make it, bake it, grow it" produce, artisan foods, handmade crafts, art, jewelry, and clothing, as well as community education, on-site services, and live entertainment.

U.S. Travel Association
1100 New York Avenue NW, Suite 450
Washington, DC 20005-3934
(202) 408-8422
Website: http://www.ustravel.org
The U.S. Travel Association is a nonprofit organization representing the travel industry in the United States.

World Federation of Tourist Guide Associations (WFTGA)
c/o Wirtschaftskammer
Stubenring 8-10
A-1010 Vienna
Austria
Website: http://www.wftga.org

The WFTGA is a nonprofit organization with over two hundred thousand individual tourist guide members in more than seventy countries. It offers education and resources to promote the professionalism and on-the-job effectiveness of tourist guides.

World Travel & Tourism Council (WTTC)
The Harlequin Building
65 Southwark Street
London SE1 0HR
United Kingdom
+44 (0) 20 7481 8007
Website: http://www.wttc.org
The WTTC raises awareness for the importance of the travel and tourism industry in the world economy. Its membership consists of travel and tourism business leaders.

Websites

Because of the changing nature of Internet links, Rosen Publishing has developed an online list of websites related to the subject of this book. This site is updated regularly. Please use this link to access the list:

http://www.rosenlinks.com/ECAR/Hosp

for further reading

Allen, Judy. *Event Planning: The Ultimate Guide to Successful Meetings, Corporate Events, Fundraising Galas, Conferences, Conventions, Incentives and Other Special Events.* Mississauga, ON: John Wiley & Sons Canada, Ltd., 2009.

Bacal, Robert. *Perfect Phrases for Customer Service*. 2nd ed. Columbus, OH: McGraw-Hill Education, 2011.

Becker, Elizabeth. *Overbooked: The Exploding Business of Travel and Tourism.* New York, NY: Simon & Schuster, 2013.

Chon, Kaye (Kye-Sung), and Thomas A. Maier. *Welcome to Hospitality: An Introduction.* Clinton Park, NY: Delmar, Cengage Learning, 2010.

de Lafayette, Maximillien. *How to Become a Perfect General Manager. Hospitality, Hotels, Restaurants, Food.* New York, NY: Times Square Press, 2011.

Ford, Robert C., Michael C. Sturman, and Cherrill P. Heaton. *Managing Quality Service in Hospitality: How Organizations Achieve Excellence in the Guest Experience.* Clinton Park, NY: Delmar, Cengage Learning, 2012.

Gallagher, Richard S. *The Customer Service Survival Kit: What to Say to Defuse Even the Worst Customer Situations.* New York, NY: AMACOM, 2013.

Gisslen, Wayne. *Professional Cooking.* Hoboken, NJ: John Wiley & Sons, Inc., 2011.

Hayes, David K., and Jack D. Ninemeier. *Human Resources Management in the Hospitality Industry.* Hoboken, NJ: John Wiley & Sons, Inc., 2009.

Hofstetter, Rachel Mount. *Cooking Up a Business: Lessons from Food Lovers Who Turned Their Passion into a Career—and How You Can, Too.* New York, NY: Penguin Group, 2013.

Hudson, Simon, and Louise Hudson. *Customer Service in Tourism and Hospitality.* Woodeaton, Oxford, England: Goodfellow Publishers, Ltd., 2012.

Inghilleri, Leonardo, and Micah Solomon. *Exceptional Service, Exceptional Profit: The Secrets of Building a Five-Star Customer Service Organization.* New York, NY: AMACOM, 2010.

Malouf, Lena. *Events Exposed: Managing and Designing Special Events.* Hoboken, NJ: John Wiley & Sons, Inc., 2012.

McCabe, Scott. *Marketing Communications in Tourism and Hospitality.* Kidlington, Oxford, England: Elsevier, Ltd., 2009.

Mohos, Mariann. *You Want WHAT??? Concierge Tales from the Men and Women Who Make Las Vegas Dreams Come True.* Seattle, WA: Amazon Digital Services, Inc., 2011.

National Restaurant Association. *ManageFirst: Customer Service with Answer Sheet.* Upper Saddle River, NJ: Prentice Hall, 2012.

Scanlon, Nancy Loman. *Catering Management.* Hoboken, NJ: John Wiley & Sons, Inc., 2013.

Scannell, Edward. *The Big Book of People Skills Games: Quick, Effective Activities for Making Great Impressions, Boosting Problem-Solving Skills and Improving Customer Service.* New York, NY: McGraw-Hill, 2010.

Solomon, Micah. *High-Tech, High-Touch Customer Service: Inspire Timeless Loyalty in the Demanding New World of Social Commerce.* New York, NY: AMACOM, 2012.

Stone, Carolyn B., and Carol A. Dahir. *School Counselor Accountability: A MEASURE of Student Success.* Upper Saddle River, NJ: Pearson Education, Inc., 2011.

Tharp, Crista. *Becoming a Wedding Planner Is Now Blissfully Simple.* Kokomo, IN: Felicity Publishing, 2013.

Tomsky, Jacob. *Heads in Beds: A Reckless Memoir of Hotels, Hustles, and So-Called Hospitality.* New York, NY: Anchor Books, 2012.

Turkel, Stanley. *Great American Hoteliers: Pioneers of the Hotel Industry.* Bloomington, IN: AuthorHouse, 2009.

bibliography

Adams, Susan. "The 10 Best Websites for Your Career–2013." Forbes.com, 2013. Retrieved January 31, 2014 (http://www.forbes.com/sites/susanadams/2013/09/18/the-10-best-websites-for-your-career 2013).

Allen, Judy. *Confessions of an Event Planner: Case Studies from the Real World of Events—How to Handle the Unexpected and How to Be a Master of Discretion.* Hoboken, NJ: Wiley Publishing, Inc., 2009.

American Hotel & Lodging Association. "2013 Lodging Industry Profile Prepared by the American Hotel & Lodging Association." Retrieved December 27, 2013. (http://www.ahla.com/content.aspx?id=35603).

Carlson, Sarah. Interview by Erin Staley. January 29, 2014.

Cran, Cheryl. *101 Ways to Make Generations X, Y and Zoomers Happy at Work.* Vancouver, BC, Canada: Synthesis at Work, Inc., 2010.

Diener, Sam. "Body Language in Different Cultures." Samdiener.com, 2009. Retrieved January 30, 2014 (http://www.samdiener.com/2009/10/body-language-in-different-cultures).

Disney Institute and Theodore Kinni. *Be Our Guest: Perfecting the Art of Customer Service.* New York, NY: Disney Editions, 2011.

Donahue, John C. "Getting Direction from the Disney Guest Service Philosophy." 2013. Retrieved January 30, 2014 (http://www.johncdonahue.com/getting-direction-from-the-disney-guest-service-philosophy).

E-importz. "Coffee Statistics 2014." Retrieved January 10, 2014 (http://www.e-importz.com/Support/specialty_coffee.htm).

Gallo, Carmine. "Customer Service the Disney Way." *Forbes*, 2011. Retrieved January 29, 2014 (http://www.forbes.com/sites/carminegallo/2011/04/14/customer-service-the-disney-way).

Krueger, Alyson. "12 Statistic-Driven Ways to Make Lasting First Impressions." *Business Insider*, 2010. Retrieved January 8, 2014 (http://www.businessinsider.com/20-ways-to-nail-a-good-first-impression-2010-12?op=1).

Lipp, Doug. *Disney U: How Disney University Develops the World's Most Engaged, Loyal, and Customer-Centric Employees.* New York, NY: McGraw-Hill, 2013.

Marriott. "J. Willard Marriott." Retrieved January 20, 2014 (http://www.marriott.com/culture-and-values/j-willard-marriott.mi).

Merriam-Webster. "Hospitality." Retrieved December 26, 2013 (http://www.merriam-webster.com/dictionary/hospitality).

Nanton, Nick, and J.W. Dicks. "Taking Direction from Disney's Customer-Care Philosophy." 2013. Retrieved January 11, 2014 (http://www.fastcompany.com/3005566/taking-direction-disneys-customer-care-philosophy).

Newsradio WTAM1100 Cleveland. "Casinos Seeing High Worker Turnover." 2013. Retrieved December 29, 2013 (http://www.wtam.com/articles/wtam-local-news-122520/casinos-seeing-high-worker-turnover-11606518).

Nightlife & Club Industry Association of America. "Our Industry." 2013. Retrieved January 31, 2014 (http://

www.nciaa.com/content.aspx?page_id=22&club_id=160641&module_id=29898).

Pedro, Lola. "Sustainable, Responsible Tourism: Luxury Travel's New Trend." *Telegraph*, 2013. Retrieved January 31, 2014 (http://www.telegraph.co.uk/luxury/travel/1983/sustainable-responsible-tourism-luxury-travels-new-trend.html).

Quijano, Elaine. "Vocational Tech Grads Buck the Jobs Trend." *CBS News*, 2011. Retrieved January 20, 2014 (http://www.cbsnews.com/news/vocational-tech-grads-buck-the-jobs-trend).

Semple, Charlotte. Interview by Erin Staley. January 29, 2014.

Silvers, Julia Rutherford. *Professional Event Coordination.* Hoboken, NJ: Wiley Publishing, Inc., 2012.

Staff of the National Estimates Branch Current Employment Statistics Survey, U.S. Bureau of Labor Statistics. "Current Employment Statistics Highlights." 2014. Retrieved January 30, 2014 (http://www.bls.gov/web/empsit/ceshighlights.pdf).

Tiebert, Laura. *Frommer's Chicago with Kids.* Hoboken, NJ: Wiley Publishing, Inc., 2009.

U.S. News & World Report. "Meeting, Convention and Event Planner." 2013. Retrieved January 28, 2014 (http://money.usnews.com/careers/best-jobs/meeting-convention-and-event-planner).

Walker, John R., and Jack E. Miller. *Supervision in the Hospitality Industry: Leading Human Resources.* Hoboken, NJ: John Wiley & Sons, Inc., 2010.

Wilson, Reid. "Hawaii's $14 Billion Tourism Industry Back to Pre-Recession." *Washington Post*, 2013. Retrieved January 30, 2014 (http://www.washingtonpost.com/blogs/govbeat/wp/2013/09/27/hawaiis-14-billion-tourism-industry-back-to-pre-recession-levels).

Wong, Alia. "Kaimuki High School Program to Prep Kids for Hospitality Industry." Civil Beat, 2013. Retrieved January 20, 2014 (http://www.civilbeat.com/articles/2013/12/16/20678-kaimuki-high-school-program-to-prep-kids-for-hospitality-industry).

World Travel & Tourism Council. "Travel & Tourism Economic Impact 2013 World." 2013. Retrieved December 24, 2013 (http://www.wttc.org/site_media/uploads/downloads/world2013_1.pdf).

index

ABOUT THE AUTHOR

The "heart of service" was engrained in Erin Staley as a youth. She cleaned homes as a high school student in Ohio and served Philly cheese steaks as a college student in New York. As an adult, she organized numerous recitals, competitions, and fund-raising events as a dance director in Oregon and managed an activities department for an all-inclusive resort in Puerto Vallarta, Mexico. Today, Staley relies on her experiences to add know-how to her expressive website content and print material for hospitality businesses in North America.

PHOTO CREDITS

Cover, p. 1 (figure) takayuki/Shuttesrtock.com; cover, p. 1 (background) The Visual Explorer/Shutterstock.com; pp. 4–5 Robert Kneschke/Shutterstock.com; pp. 8–9 Bloomberg/Getty Images; pp. 10–11 Tim Mosenfelder/Getty Images; p. 12 Steve Debenport/E+/Getty Images; pp. 14–15 Gabriel Bouys/AFP/Getty Images; p. 17 nakamasa Shutterstock.com; pp. 18–19 Larry W. Smith/EPA/Landov; p. 22 Golden Pixels LLC/Shutterstock.com; pp. 24–25 pio3/Shutterstock.com; pp. 26–27 China Photos/Shutterstock.com; pp. 28–29 Jupiterimages/Photolibrary/Getty Images; pp. 32–33 Erik Dreyer/The Image Bank/Getty Images; pp. 34–35 Monkey Business Images/Stockbyte/Getty Images; pp. 36–37 SergiyN/Shutterstock.com; p. 38--39 Image Source/Getty Images; pp. 40 © 2014 NBA Entertainment. Photo by David Dow/NBAE/Getty Images; pp. 42–43 Catarina Belova/Shutterstock.com; pp. 44–45 G. K./Shutterstock.com; p. 48 Michael DeLeon/E+/Getty Images; p. 53 Ma Ping/Xinhua/Landov; p. 57 courtesy Sarah Carlson, The Red Hare Personal Chef; pp.58–59 Eugene Kalenkovich/Shutterstock.com; p. 61 Charlotte Semple.

Designer: Matt Cauli; Photo Researcher: Marty Levick